Animal Adaptations

Behavior

STEVE GOLDSWORTHY

AV² provides enriched content that supplements and complements this book. Weigl's AV² books strive to create inspired learning and engage young minds in a total learning experience.

Your AV² Media Enhanced books come alive with...

Audio
Listen to sections of the book read aloud.

Key Words
Study vocabulary, and complete a matching word activity.

Video
Watch informative video clips.

Quizzes
Test your knowledge.

Go to **www.av2books.com**, and enter this book's unique code.

Embedded Weblinks
Gain additional information for research.

Slide Show
View images and captions, and prepare a presentation.

BOOK CODE

M 2 3 3 9 9 2

AV² by Weigl brings you media enhanced books that support active learning.

Try This!
Complete activities and hands-on experiments.

... and much, much more!

Published by AV² by Weigl
350 5th Avenue, 59th Floor
New York, NY 10118
Websites: www.av2books.com   www.weigl.com

Library of Congress Control Number: 2014941761
ISBN 978-1-4896-1366-0 (hardcover)
ISBN 978-1-4896-1367-7 (softcover)
ISBN 978-1-4896-1368-4 (single-user eBook)
ISBN 978-1-4896-1369-1 (multi-user eBook)

Printed in the United States of America in North Mankato, Minnesota
1 2 3 4 5 6 7 8 9 18 17 16 15 14

062014
WEP050914

Project Coordinator Aaron Carr
Art Director Terry Paulhus

Every reasonable effort has been made to trace ownership and to obtain permission to reprint copyright material. The publishers would be pleased to have any errors or omissions brought to their attention so that they may be corrected in subsequent printings.

Photo Credits
Weigl acknowledges Getty Images as its primary photo supplier for this title.

Contents

What Is an Adaptation?

An adaptation is any change to an animal that helps it survive in a particular **habitat**. Some animals are born with adaptations. Other animals learn adaptive behavior from their parents. These adaptations can be passed on to the next generation. In this way, adaptations help in the survival of the **species**.

A particular species will continue to survive through a process called **natural selection**. Animals that have developed useful adaptations survive and pass their adaptations to their young.

Chimpanzees use sticks to fish for termites. The ability to use tools is an example of an adaptation.

5 AMAZING ADAPTATIONS

Animals adapt for many reasons, including extreme temperatures, to avoid **predators**, movement, to find food, and to find a **mate**.

Hibernation

Some animals have developed the ability to enter long periods of very deep sleep during cold winter months. This is called hibernation. North American box turtles can hibernate for 150 days. During hibernation, they do not even breathe. Instead, they take in oxygen through their skin.

Migration

As seasons change, many animals move areas. This movement, known as migration, may be in search of warmer weather or new feeding grounds. During the winter, gray whales migrate thousands of miles (kilometers). They swim from the Arctic down to the warm waters of Mexico.

Tool Use

Some animals have learned how to make and use tools they find in their habitat. Sea otters use sharp stones to break open molluscs to eat. They will often carry these stones around with them.

Food Storage

Many animals have learned to adapt to a lack of food during the winter by storing food in the fall. Beavers build food piles of tree branches. They can eat the bark of these branches even while their pond is frozen.

Burrowers

Some animals have adapted to cold or hot environments by living underground. The naked mole rat has adapted to the heat of the East African desert by burrowing. It has learned to dig tunnels through the cool earth.

What Is a Behavioral Adaptation?

A behavioral adaptation is a change in the way an animal acts in reaction to its habitat. A habitat might be cold or hot. An animal must learn to seek shelter from the harsh weather. There might be a shortage of food during a particular season. Animals will have to learn to store food ahead of time. They may also have to hibernate to avoid food shortages during the winter. Some animals will have to learn how to hunt at night if their **prey** is **nocturnal**.

MIGRATION

Migration is a very common behavioral adaptation. Many species of birds migrate throughout the year. They begin in a warm region known as their breeding ground. This is a place where birds mate, hatch their eggs, and raise their young.

A change in the climate tells migrating animals it is time to move. As it gets colder, **scarcity** of food becomes an issue. Birds will take their young with them as they fly south for the winter.

✿ 🍁 MIGRATION OF THE PEREGRINE FALCON

The **tundra** peregrine falcon has one of the longest migrations of any bird in North America. It spends the spring and summer in the Arctic before flying south for the winter. The tundra peregrine falcon will fly up to 15,500 miles (25,000 km) in a year!

Peregrine falcons feed and raise their young during the spring and summer months. As the temperatures drop, they prepare for their journey south. Young falcons observe their parents and learn when it is time to migrate.

✿
Spring

In the fall, the falcons begin their 8- to 14-week journey to South America for the winter. They cover an average of 150 miles (241 km) each day. The birds stop along the way to feed and rest.

🍁
Fall

What Does It Do?

Behavioral adaptations help an animal to survive in a particular habitat. Grizzly bears have learned to catch salmon in rivers. They stand in the middle of flowing water as large salmon swim upstream. They have learned to rely on the salmon's **instinct** to swim upstream to its breeding ground.

Grizzly bear cubs learn how to fish by watching their mother.

STORING FOOD

Natural selection is an important part in the development of all species. It involves animals adapting to their environments. For example, many animals react to changes in the temperature of their environment. Animals such as squirrels have developed the ability to store food for the winter. They hide nuts in the ground during fall. They can later return to where they hid their food when there is less food to find.

An animal that has adapted its behavior to its environment will be more successful. It can eat, move around, and find a mate easier. It can then pass on these adaptations to its offspring.

FOOD PYRAMID

Adaptation plays an important role for all animals in a **food pyramid**.

Tertiary Consumers are large animals that eat smaller animals for food. The grizzly bear is a tertiary consumer. It has learned how to hunt for prey from its parents. It has adapted to hibernation during the winter months. Grizzly bears mostly eat plants, but they also eat fish, squirrels, and other animals.

Secondary Consumers are small animals that feed on primary consumers. Squirrels are secondary consumers as they are known to eat insects such as grasshoppers. They have adapted to their environment by learning to store nuts and seeds for when food is hard to find in the winter. They also hibernate when food is scarce.

Primary Consumers are insects and other small animals that eat plants for food. Grasshoppers are a primary consumer. They have learned to migrate to areas where there is more food. They will also swarm together in large numbers. This keeps them organized and can protect some of them from predators.

Producers use energy from the sun to make their own food. Some animals eat producers. This passes energy to the next level of the pyramid. In this way, producers support the entire food pyramid.

Types of Behavioral Adaptations

There are two main types of behavioral adaptation, learned and instinctual. Some behavioral adaptations are learned from an animal's parents. Sometimes animals learn by observing others in their group. Other behavioral adaptations are instinctual. This means an animal is born with the behavior.

Packs of wolves have learned to work together in groups of four or five to hunt prey.

2 WAYS ANIMALS ADAPT THEIR BEHAVIOR

Learned Behavior

Some birds migrate to warmer habitats during the winter. They have learned where to fly from traveling with their parents.

Chimpanzees learn how to hunt in packs from their group members. They will call to one another and work as a team. Young chimps learn the calls and hunting techniques.

Instinctual Behavior

A spider has developed the ability to spin a web to catch its food. It knows how to do this without being taught by its parents.

Moles have adapted to life underground. They are born with the ability to dig tunnels in search of food.

How Does It Work?

Animals develop most behavioral adaptations to suit their habitat. Animals will either adapt to conditions in their habitat, or they will leave. If the change is seasonal, they will usually come back once the habitat warms up. Changes in weather force an animal to migrate to a different climate. Scarcity of a particular food source forces an animal to change its diet. Animals either learn these behavioral adaptations from their parents, or they are born with them, which is called instinct.

Japanese macaques have learned to warm themselves in natural hot springs.

4 DIFFERENT ENVIRONMENTS ANIMALS HAVE ADAPTED TO

Desert

Kangaroo rats have adapted to life in the hot, dry deserts of the United States. They build underground burrows where they stay during the day.

Night

Many animals have adapted their behaviors to being active at night. Bats adapted to night hunting to avoid competition from birds. They have adapted to hunting other nocturnal creatures such as moths.

High Mountains

Many animals live at extremely high **elevations**. Some mountain ranges are so high, the air is very thin. Red foxes living in the Andean Mountains of South America have adapted to the thin air. They sneak up on their prey instead of chasing it. By conserving energy, they need less oxygen.

Antarctic

Penguins have developed ways to survive in extreme cold. They huddle together in large groups to protect themselves from cold wind, taking turns on the outside of the group.

Timeline

Earth has changed in many ways over millions of years. About 200 million years ago, **continents** began to form. They broke away from each other, changing the habitat of many animals. Birds have been migrating throughout the world for many millions of years. As the continents shifted, birds were forced to adapt their migrating habits. Africa and Asia were once connected. As the continents drifted apart, bird species that migrated between these two continents had to travel farther and farther away.

One of the strongest influences on the migration of birds has been the temperature of Earth. It has warmed up and cooled down many times for millions of years. During this time, several **ice ages** have occurred. Continental ice sheets covered thousands of square miles of land in Northern Europe and North America. When temperatures warmed, these ice sheets melted and moved north. Colder temperatures allowed the ice sheets to spread south again. Birds had to adapt constantly to these shifts in ice sheets.

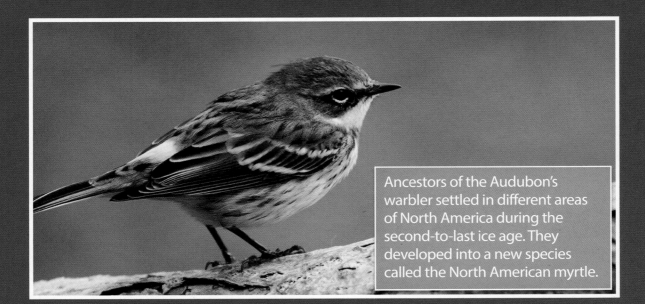

Ancestors of the Audubon's warbler settled in different areas of North America during the second-to-last ice age. They developed into a new species called the North American myrtle.

Adaptations of the Audubon's Warbler Over Time

180,000 Years Ago

The entire top half of North America was covered in a **glacier**. This glacier then spread south. Ancestral species of birds were pushed out of their traditional habitats in the north. They had to establish new nesting grounds as far south as present-day Mexico. They migrated far down into South America during warmer seasons.

120,000 Years Ago

The temperature of Earth warmed up. The ice sheet moved north to a position similar to where it is today. Bird species such as the Audubon's warbler were able to re-establish their ancient nesting grounds. They continued to migrate to spots in the southern United States.

48,000 Years Ago

The last ice age brought an ice sheet that reached as far south as present-day northern Nebraska. Many animals were forced from their habitats once again. The Audubon's warbler returned to nesting grounds at the bottom of North America. At this time, other species of warblers emerged and established themselves in southern regions.

Today

The modern day Audubon's warbler has established nesting grounds as far north as Alaska. These birds continue to migrate to some areas in Mexico, but spend a lot of the winter in the northern United States. Bird species such as the warbler continue to adapt to the changing climate of Earth.

Copying Behavioral Adaptations

People use unique adaptations from the animal world to invent many things. From observing how animals have adapted, scientists have developed very useful technology. Engineers and inventors have created many tools and equipment based on this technology.

Beavers have adapted to living on rivers and streams. They have learned to build dams and channel water. Engineers have based the design of new hydroelectricity dams on beaver dams. Hydroelectricity dams use the energy of running water to make power. By making dams smaller, people can still produce electricity with less impact on the environment than caused by dams of the past.

Beaver dams are good for wetland habitats. They slow the flow of streams, which creates still ponds suitable for fish nurseries.

Spiders have learned to build webs that are extremely strong. Engineers have studied the design of spider webs. They hope to develop technology that is similar to a spider's web. This technology would help to build stronger structures such as bridges and buildings.

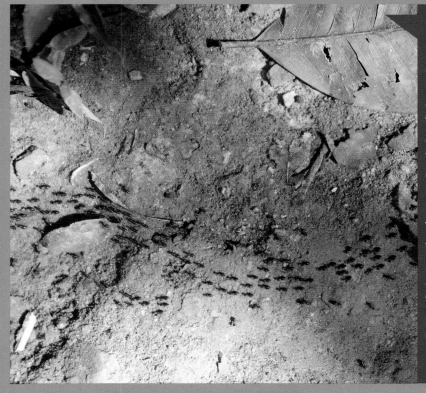

Ants can create a trail between their colony and a food source. They find the shortest path and are able to leave a trail for other ants. In the early 1990s, computer scientists studied these patterns of behavior. They created a system for computers to solve problems based on ant behavior. Today, this technology helps people do searches on the internet.

Behavioral Adaptations and Biodiversity

Biodiversity refers to the variety of life forms in a particular habitat or biome. Biomes are areas around the world where specific climates and plants exist. This includes aquatic (water), desert, forest, and grasslands. Animals living in biomes have adapted to these specific environments.

To find their own place in a habitat, many animals must develop unique behavioral adaptations. When several species live closely together, each species specializes. For instance, several species of cichlid fish live together in Africa's Lake Malawi. They do not compete for food, however. One species eats only insects while another eats only fish or algae.

The Great Barrier Reef, off the coast of Australia, is known for its biodiversity. The reef is home to dugongs, six of the world's seven species of marine turtle, more than 1,500 species of fish, and many other kinds of aquatic life.

SWARMING

A common behavioral adaptation is swarming. Large numbers of animals move together in a group. Some animals have learned to communicate as a swarm.

Thousands of honeybees live together in a hive. When the group gets too large, they must move.

This tells the queen bee and the other bees where to build the new hive.

Scouts fly out and find a new spot to build a hive. When a suitable spot is chosen, other bees come out to see it.

If selected, the bees will swarm there in a large group.

Conservation

The process of adaptation can take hundreds of thousands of years. Many animals have adapted to their habitats in such a special way they cannot survive anywhere else. If their environment is changed, even slightly, it could lead to their extinction.

Climate change can have a destructive effect. As the planet heats up, biomes such as the frozen tundra will shrink. Animals that have adapted to life there may be forced to leave, or die out.

The migratory patterns of birds can easily be upset. Many species of birds, such as the ruddy turnstone, stop over on their way to their southern habitats. They settle in Delaware Bay, New Jersey, and fill up on horseshoe crab. People in the area also fish for horseshoe crab. This threatens one of the main food sources of turnstones.

Wildlife groups are working hard with governments and industry to save natural areas around the world. Protected **ecosystems** include tropical rainforests, coral reefs, and freshwater river systems.

Ruddy turnstones are often seen on human-made structures or equipment along coasts.

Activity

Match the animal with the behavioral characteristic that helps it survive.

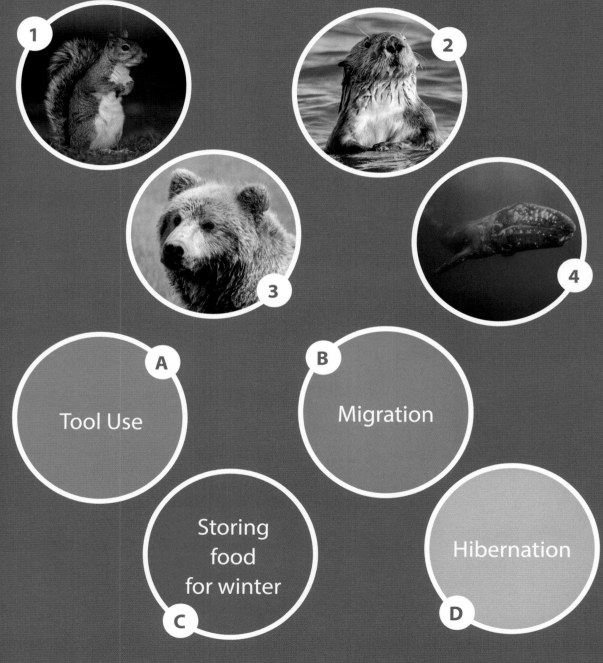

A Tool Use

B Migration

C Storing food for winter

D Hibernation

Quiz

Complete this quiz to test your knowledge of behavioral adaptations.

1 How long can North American box turtles hibernate for?

A. 150 days

2 What animal uses a stone to break open molluscs to eat?

A. Sea otter

3 How do naked mole rats stay cool in the deserts of East Africa?

A. They dig tunnels.

4 How many miles can a peregrine falcon cover each day during its migration?

A. 150 miles (241 km)

5 What are the two main types of behavioral adaptation?

A. Learned and instinctual

6 What is one way penguins have learned to stay warm in Antarctica?

A. They huddle together.

7 What major events forced ancestral birds to develop their migratory habits?

A. Ice ages

8 What was the main inspiration for engineers to develop new hydroelectric dams?

A. Beaver dams

9 What behavioral adaptation do honeybees use to communicate?

A. Swarming

10 Name one protected ecosystem.

A. Tropical rainforests, coral reefs, and freshwater river systems

Key Words

continents: the world's main large areas of land (Europe, Asia, Africa, North and South America, Australia, Antarctica)

ecosystems: communities of living things and their environments

elevations: altitudes or heights of mountain regions

food pyramid: a pyramid-shaped diagram of a food chain, with producers at the bottom and end consumers at the top

glacier: a very slow-moving mass of ice formed from hard packed snow

habitat: the natural environment of a living thing

ice ages: periods of time with extreme cold and glaciers

instinct: a way of behaving that an animal is born with

mate: a breeding partner

natural selection: a natural process where animals that have better adapted to their environment survive and pass on those adaptations to their young

nocturnal: animals who are most active at night

predators: animals that hunt and eat other animals

prey: animals that are hunted and eaten by other animals

scarcity: a shortage of something, such as food

species: a group of plants or animals that are alike in many ways

tundra: a vast, frozen, treeless area of ice and snow

Index

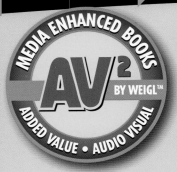

Log on to www.av2books.com

AV² by Weigl brings you media enhanced books that support active learning. Go to www.av2books.com, and enter the special code found on page 2 of this book. You will gain access to enriched and enhanced content that supplements and complements this book. Content includes video, audio, weblinks, quizzes, a slide show, and activities.

AV² Online Navigation

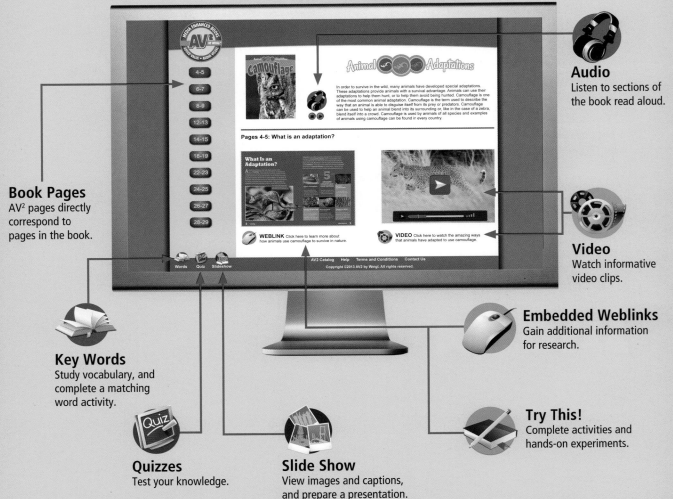

Audio
Listen to sections of the book read aloud.

Book Pages
AV² pages directly correspond to pages in the book.

Video
Watch informative video clips.

Key Words
Study vocabulary, and complete a matching word activity.

Embedded Weblinks
Gain additional information for research.

Quizzes
Test your knowledge.

Slide Show
View images and captions, and prepare a presentation.

Try This!
Complete activities and hands-on experiments.

AV² was built to bridge the gap between print and digital. We encourage you to tell us what you like and what you want to see in the future.

Sign up to be an AV² Ambassador at www.av2books.com/ambassador.